This **Book** Belongs To **Future STEM** Leader:

____

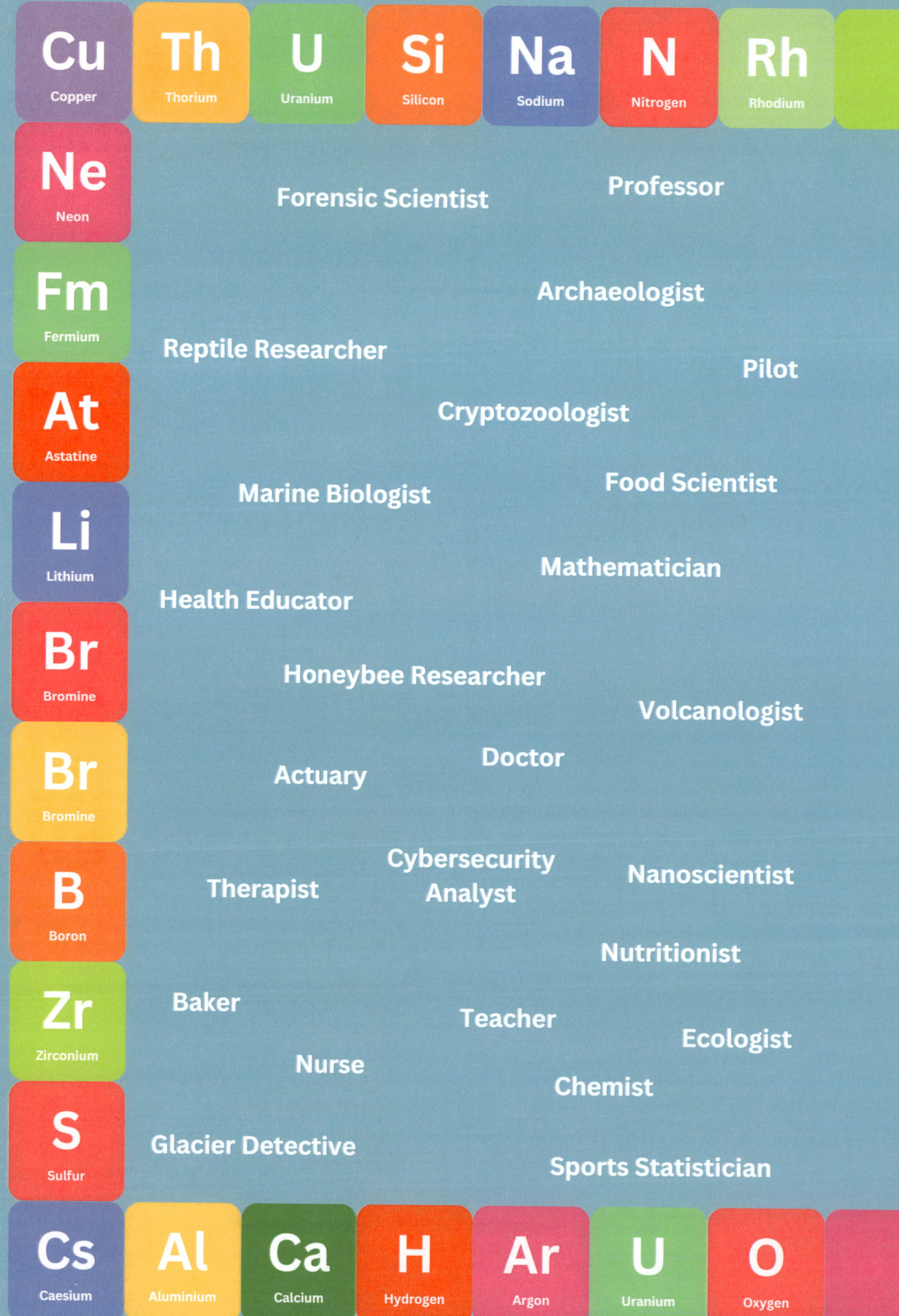

Cu
Copper
Th
Thorium
U
Uranium
Si
Silicon
Na
Sodium
N
Nitrogen
Rh
Rhodium
Ne
Neon
Fm
Fermium
At
Astatine
Li
Lithium
Br
Bromine
Br
Bromine
B
Boron
Zr
Zirconium
S
Sulfur
Cs
Caesium
Al
Aluminium
Ca
Calcium
H
Hydrogen
Ar
Argon
U
Uranium
O
Oxygen
Forensic Scientist
Professor
Archaeologist
Reptile Researcher
Pilot
Cryptozoologist
Marine Biologist
Food Scientist
Mathematician
Health Educator
Honeybee Researcher
Volcanologist
Doctor
Actuary
Cybersecurity Analyst
Nanoscientist
Therapist
Nutritionist
Baker
Teacher
Ecologist
Nurse
Chemist
Glacier Detective
Sports Statistician

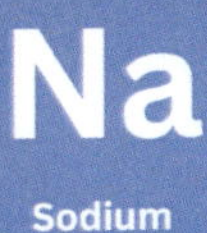

Na Sodium

C Carbon

Tl Thallium

Cf Californium

He Helium

Ra Radium

Rh Rhodium

Cm Curium

Si Silicon

I Iodine

Zn Zinc

U Uranium

K Potassium

Ca Calcium

Rn Radon

B Boron

STEM Inspires Me

Look Inside So You Can See

Fragrance Chemist

Botanist

Sports Engineer

Medical Illustrator

Movie Animator

Pyrotechnic Engineer

Whale Detective

Cartoonist

Astronaut

Policy Advisor

Storm Tracker

Ice Cream Specialist

Pastry Chef

Surgeon

Dentist

Data Scientist

Climatologist

Veterinary Dentist

Engineer

P Phosphorus

Mn Manganese

Be Beryllium

Pb Lead

Fe Iron

O Oxygen

Hg Mercury

STEM Inspires Me: Look Inside So You Can See
First Edition

This book is written to inspire, educate, and motivate children about science, technology, engineering, and mathematics in a fun, culturally diverse way.

Editing by Jasmine Wilson

Illustrations by Princess Karibo

Formatted by Favour Yakubu

For school STEM visits,
please contact Author Creea Shannon at:

authorcreeashannon@gmail.com

STEM Inspires Me

Look Inside So You Can See

Written by Creea Shannon

Dedicated to the Youth:

Use your imagination, never be limited by another person's limited imagination, and always DREAM BIG!

- Creea 

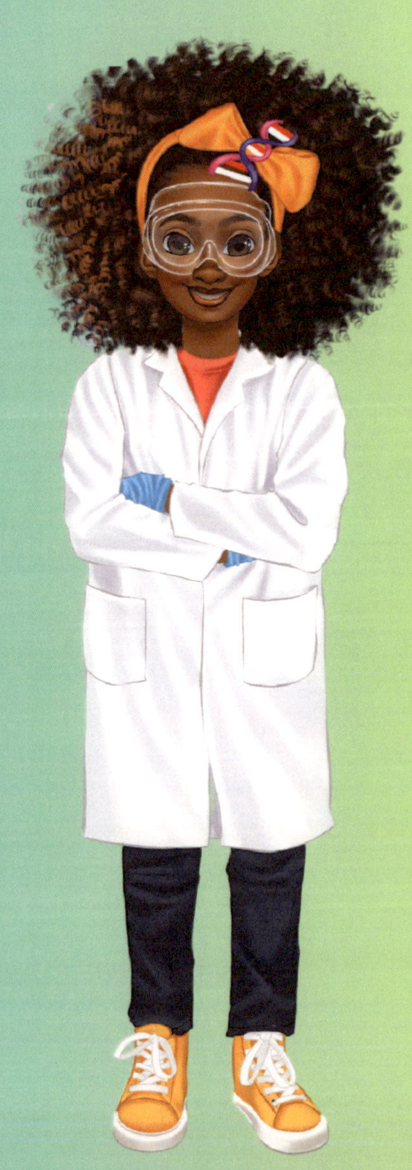

My name is Cre, and I want the world to know what
inspires me. . .

STEM!

STEM!

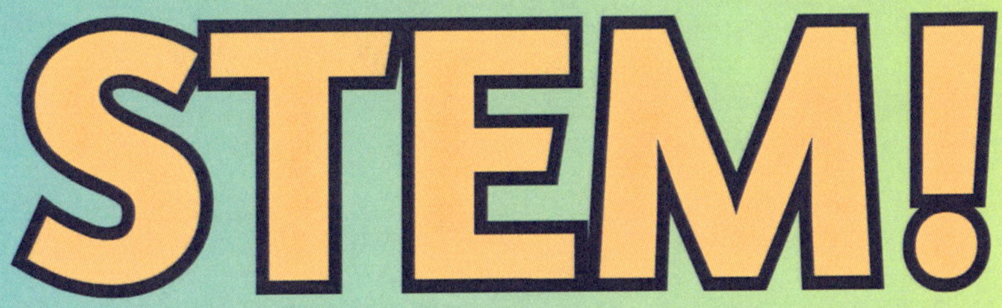

stands for

S - Science

T - Technology

E - Engineering and

M - Mathematics

Science is the study of the world around us. Through observations and experiments, scientists such as **Funmi** discover new things. They look for ways to keep our air clean, analyze DNA to solve crimes, and they perform research that helps to create more ways to cure people of certain diseases.

Funmi the Scientist

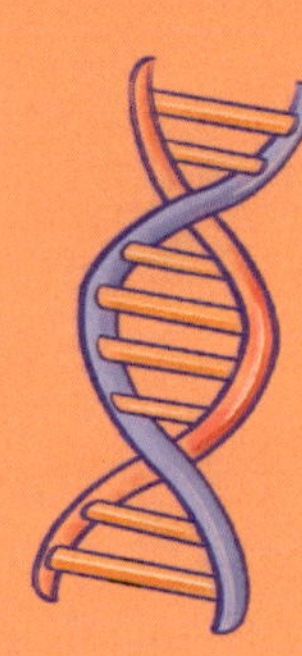

Science helps answer questions such as. . .
Why do popsicles melt?
How do volcanoes form?
Where does snow come from?

Science Fact:
A rainbow is actually a complete circle, not an arc. From the ground, we only see a semi-circle.

In SCIENCE, I'm inspired to be. . .
A Zoologist, who studies animals and how they interact with the ecosystem.
Sage the Zoologist

Technology is applying science to solve a problem. Technology can make everyday activities more effective and fun.

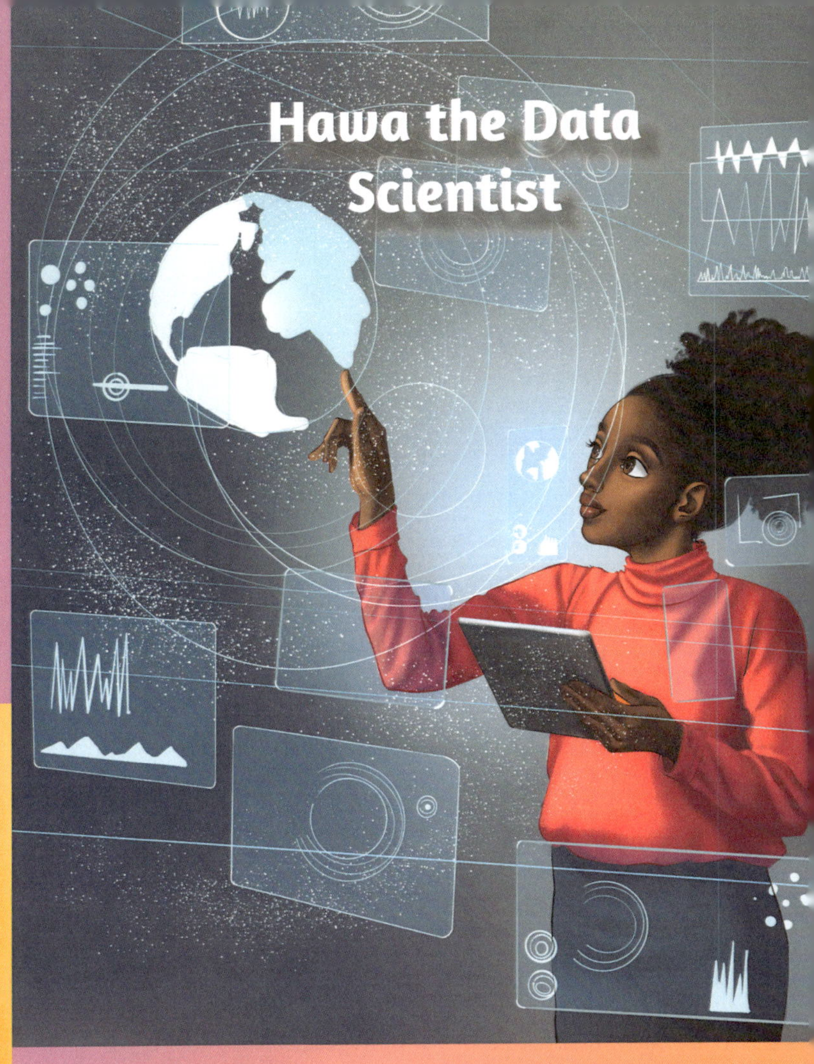

Amasyah the DJ

We can use different gadgets and devices such as an iPad, cellphone, or computer to listen to music or watch our favorite show.

Tech Fact:
Technology in music can help people remember things even if they have had a serious brain injury.

In TECHNOLOGY, I'm inspired to be. . .

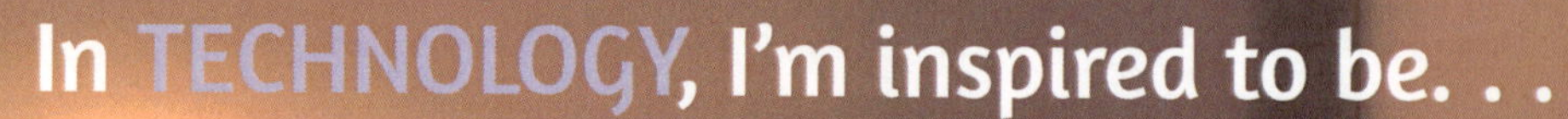

A Video Game Designer, who creates characters, storylines, game levels, and other fun parts of a game. They bring video games to life.

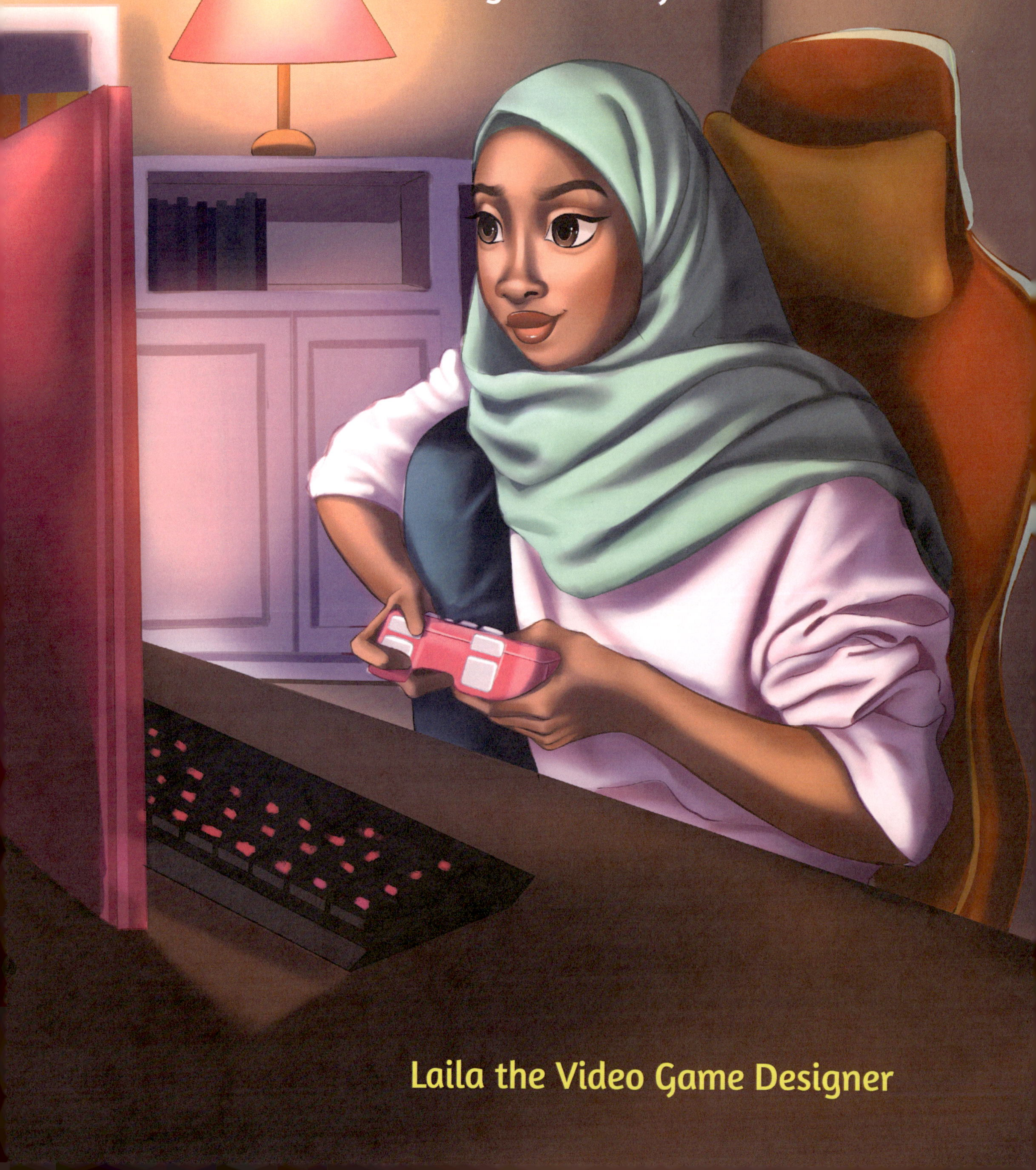

Laila the Video Game Designer

Engineering is used to solve some of the world's biggest challenges by designing and building things.

Engineers can create **artificial limbs** for people with disabilities, and they construct playgrounds for children to swing and play on.

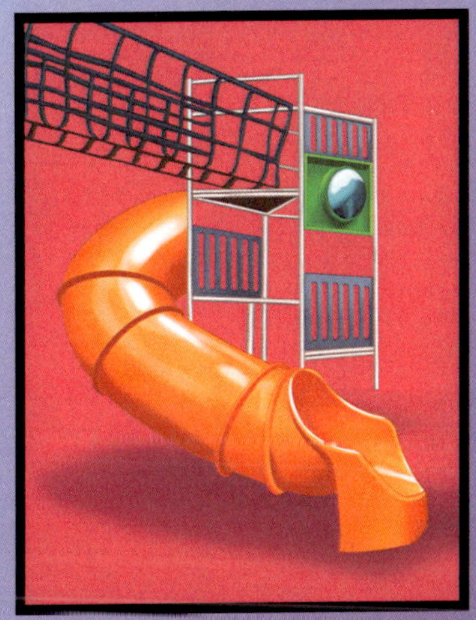

Engineers also find ways to protect the Earth from water and air pollution.

Engineering Fact:
Engineers create robots to help doctors during surgeries.

In ENGINEERING, I'm inspired to be. . .
A Biomedical Engineer, who uses biology, engineering, and medicine to improve the functions of the human body and design medical equipment such as prosthetic limbs.
Oyana the Engineer

Mathematics is the study of numbers and science that deals with shapes, quantity, and arrangements.

Math is all around us—in everything we do. It's used in software, money, architecture, and even sports. Math is essential in **basketball** to improve a player's performance while shooting.

We also use math when baking our favorite cookies or cupcakes by adding, subtracting, and measuring ingredients.

Math Fact:

Ancient Egyptians used math to build pyramids.

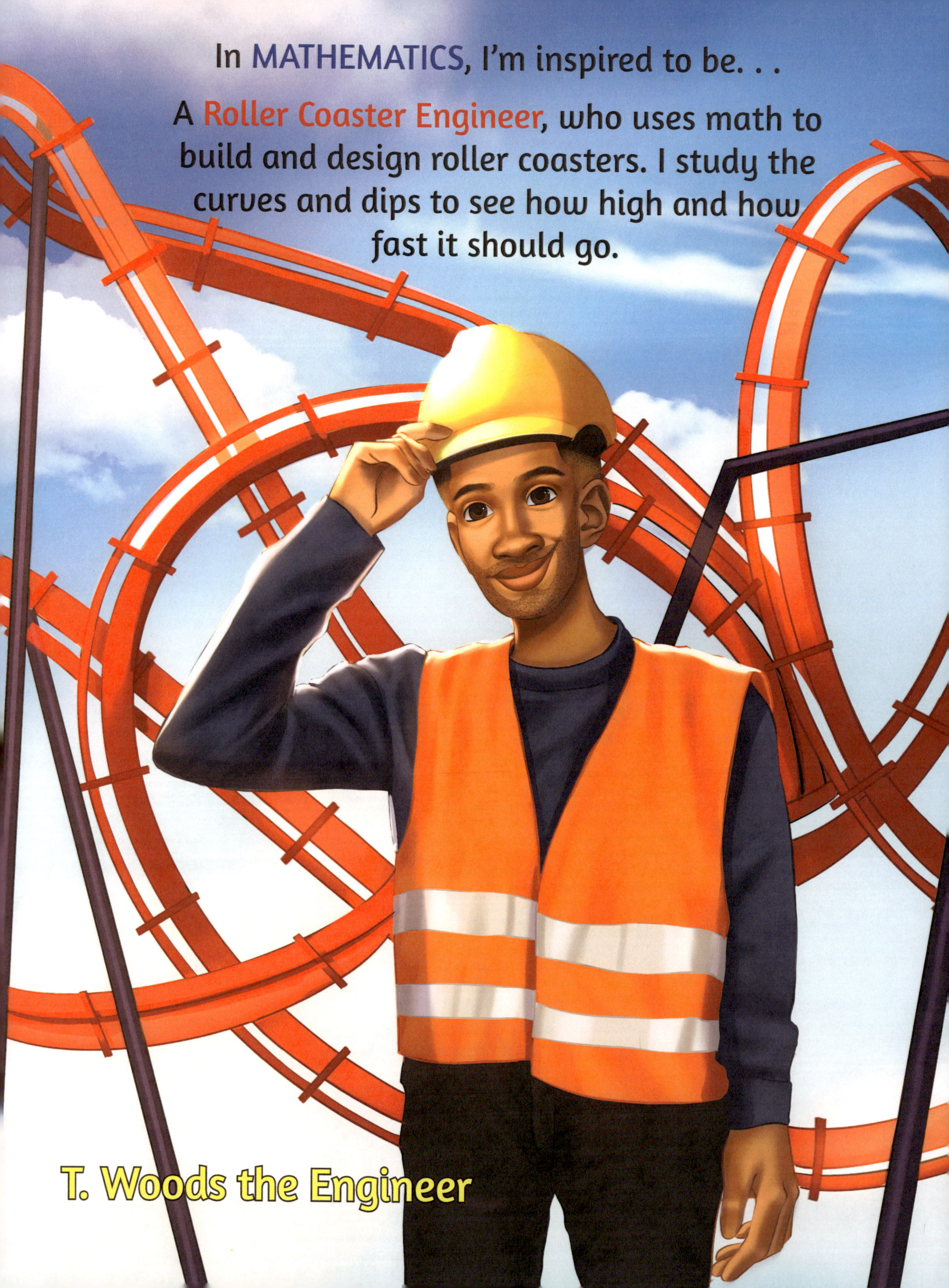

In MATHEMATICS, I'm inspired to be. . .
A Roller Coaster Engineer, who uses math to build and design roller coasters. I study the curves and dips to see how high and how fast it should go.
T. Woods the Engineer

STEM inspires me to be so many amazing things!
Meet my STEM friends and see what STEM inspires them to be!

I'm Sam, I am inspired to be a Forensic Scientist who uses DNA, fingerprints, and blood to investigate crime scenes.

I'm Priya, I am inspired to be an Aeronautical Engineer,
who designs and creates drones, planes, and helicopters.

I'm **Akila**, I am inspired to be a Food Scientist, who uses science to make food yummier, healthier, and safer.

I'm Johanna, I am inspired to be a Marine Ecologist, who studies living things in the ocean and how they interact in the environment. They work with animals such as fish, crustaceans, whales, dolphins, and reptiles.

I'm Nadia, I am inspired to be a Virologist, who studies tiny invaders known as viruses. They research what viruses do in our bodies.

I'm Layo, I am inspired to be a Astronaut, who embark on journeys to space and discover the fascinating mysteries beyond our planet Earth.

I'm Rosa, I am inspired to be an Archaeologist, who analyzes artifacts such as buildings, tools, weapons, art, and more to understand cultures.

I'm Bina, I am inspired to be a Honey Bee Researcher who study beehives and bees as they collect nectar and turn it into sweet, delicious honey. They make sure bees thrive to pollinate fruit and vegetables.

I'm Neve, I am inspired to be a Climatologist, who studies the atmosphere and analyzes data research to understand climate issues.

I'm Shaka, I am inspired to be a Sports Statistician Analyst, who analyzes data for sporting events, usually for major sports such as baseball, football or basketball.

I'm Maria, I am inspired to be a Civil Engineer, who designs and constructs buildings, roads, and bridges.

There are so many reasons **STEM** inspires me. If you **DREAM BIG** sky will be the limit on what you can be!

What does STEM Inspire YOU
to be?

Other Ways to Inspire...

1. Give back and uplift others
2. Read with children in underserved communities
3. Start a community project
4. Help a senior citizen
5. Have an attitude of gratitude
6. Let your voice be heard
7. Believe in Yourself!

Scientist

Technologist

Engineer

Mathematician

37 Inspiring, Diverse Figures in STEM

Henrietta Lacks, Mother of Modern Medicine—Her cervical cancer cells are the source of the HeLa cell line.

Jane Cooke Wright—Mother of Chemotherapy and a cancer researcher.

Jewel Plummer Cobb—Biologist and cancer researcher who was effective in the treatment of certain skin cancers, lung cancers, and childhood leukemia.

Patricia Bath—Ophthalmologist and laser scientist.

Kalpana Chawla—Flight engineer and Columbia Mission specialist she was the first Indian woman to go to space.

Irene Uchida—Japanese Canadian geneticist and Down syndrome researcher, who introduced cytogenetics and advanced the study of chromosomes in Canada.

Sir John Cornforth—Australian British Chemist who achieved a Nobel Prize for his contributions to the stereochemistry of enzyme-catalysed reactions, despite being deaf.

Hedy Lamarr—Austrian-American actress and inventor who created "frequency hopping" that helped make it possible for Wi-Fi, GPS, and bluetooth communication systems.

Sarah Stewart—Mexican-American researcher, made a groundbreaking discovery connecting viruses to cancer, thereby laying the foundation for the creation of vaccines aimed at protecting against specific forms of the disease.

Marie Maynard Daly—First black woman to obtain a Ph.D. in chemistry.

Ellen Ochoa—Astronaut and first Hispanic woman to travel to space.

Maha Al Mozaini—Scientist and founder of the first HIV/AIDS laboratory in Saudi Arabia.

Rebecca Lee Crumpler—First African-American woman to become a medical doctor in the United States.

June Bacon-Bercey—First African-American woman to become a meteorologist.

Grace Hopper—Computer scientist and naval officer who revolutionized early computer programming languages.

Christine Darden—Mathematician, data analyst, and aeronautical engineer.

Mae Jemison—NASA astronaut, the first black woman to travel into space when she served as a mission specialist aboard the space shuttle Endeavour.

Jane Goodall—British ethologist, raised awareness of the challenges of chimpanzees and wildlife, advocating for their protection and conservation of natural habitats.

Yvonne Young Clark—First woman to receive a Bachelor of Science degree in mechanical engineering from Howard University.

Alma Levant Hayden—Chemist, and one of the first African-American women to gain a scientist position at a science agency.

Jonny Kim—Astronaut and Navy lieutenant.

Bessie Blount Griffin—Invented a feeding device and taught amputee veterans to write with their teeth and feet. She was also a forensic handwriting analyst.

Mabel Keaton Staupers—Registered nurse who improved the status of Black nurses and promoted better health care for Black Americans.

Carolyn Beatrice Parker—First African American to earn a postgraduate degree in physics at MIT.

Gladys West—Mathematician who created the GPS system.

Josephine Silone Yates—First black woman to head a college science department.

Janina Jeff—Population geneticist and bioinformatics scientist, the first African American to earn a PhD in Human Genetics from Vanderbilt University.

Antonia C. Novello—First Hispanic woman to serve as U.S. Surgeon General.

Sharon McDougle—NASA suit technician and first CEE Crew Chief.

Alexa Irene Canady—First Black woman neurosurgeon in the U.S.

Mariam Daniel Mann—One of the first "human computers" that made major contributions at NASA.

Henry Lowe—Jamaican scientist who discovered bioactive molecules from medicinal plants for possible treatment of cancer and diabetes.

Tiffani Bright—The first African-American woman to graduate with a PhD in Biomedical Informatics from Columbia University.

Shirley Ann Jackon—Physicist and inventor of the touch-tone telephone.

Annie Easley—Mathematician, computer scientist and rocket scientist who contributed to space exploration and advancement of diversity and inclusion in STEM fields.

Ronald McNair—Physicist and astronaut who was the second African American to make flight into space. He was one of seven crew members who lost their lives in the 1986 Space Shuttle Challenger explosion.

Asia Cottom—Eleven year old STEM scholar who lost her life on 9/11 while on Flight #77. The Asia Cottom Memorial Scholarship Foundation has supported many STEM students throughout college. May her impact in STEM be remembered.

Cultural Meaning of Character Names

1. Funmi - West African Yoruba, God gives me joy and happiness
2. Sage - Latin, wise
3. Hawa - Hebrew, Swahili, form of Eve
4. Amasyah - Hebrew, God is powerful, and he watches over me
5. Laila - Arabic, of the night
6. Oyana - Kenyan, uplift and inspire
7. Priya - Sanskrit, beloved
8. Akila - Latin, intelligent
9. Johanna - German/Hebrew, God is gracious
10. Nadia - Russian, hope
11. Maria - Spanish, rebellion
12. Layo - West African Yoruba, joy and happiness
13. Rosa - Spanish, rose
14. Bina - Hebrew, knowledge and insight
15. Neve - Irish, snow and radiant
16. Shaka - African, powerful

Embracing diverse culture in STEM literacy is essential for fostering innovation, inclusivity, and a more comprehensive understanding of the world's challenges. Increasing cultural visibility in STEM is vital to help youth to see themselves in the stories shared. It's a pivotal catalyst for progress, exerting a positive influence on both society and the future of science, technology, engineering, and mathematics.

ABOUT THE AUTHOR

Creea Shannon is a STEM, health, and underserved advocate. She is the mother of two little ones. She has a bachelor's and master's degree in biochemistry and second master's in data science. She's currently a PhD student at Vanderbilt University studying biomedical informatics. Her goals are to tackle health disparities and genetic variations affecting minorities by applying computational biological research methods with precision medicine and genomics. Creea wants to help increase diversity in research, which is necessary to bridge the gap in healthcare disparities.

Creea believes that youth need to know that their ideas are limitless.

"Reading is a gift every child deserves."

-Creea

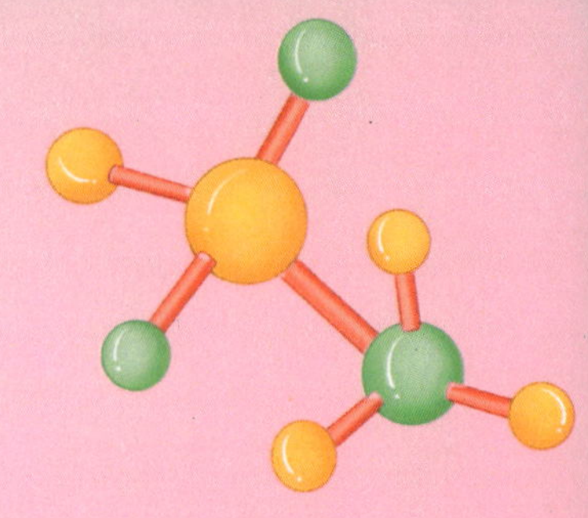

My "Why" for Writing

STEM Inspires ME:

Reading to youth in underserved elementary schools inspired me to write this book. Children should be able to see themselves in books, but there is a lack of representation.
Reading can lead to empowerment and endless possibilities.

I'm now passionate and on a mission to break the barriers of representation in STEM and literature. I hope my book, "STEM Inspires Me" encourages children to use their imaginations and Dream BIG!!

-Creea

ABOUT THE ILLUSTRATOR

Princess Karibo is a self-taught illustrator from Nigeria. She enjoys bringing her ideas to life through illustration. Most of her work is representational and focuses on giving black women a voice in the way that she can. Princess has illustrated a number of children's books aiming to empower young readers and influence the way young girls around the world see themselves.

Connect with Creea on Social Media:

Website: authorcreeashannon.com
IG: @journey2_drshannon
For more STEM, health, and medicine
@we.are.medicine
Email: authorcreeashannon@gmail.com
Twitter: @Cre_Shannon
TikTok: cre_shannon

Post a photo of you and your book with the hashtag
#STEMInspiresMe